Copyright © 2026 Lancee Whetman

ISBN: 979-8-9897302-2-3

Visit the author's website at www.vigilancee.org & on Instagram @__vigilancee.

All rights reserved. No part of this publication may be reproduced, distributed, or transmitted in any form or by any means, including photocopying, recording, or other electronic or mechanical methods, without the prior written permission of the publisher or author, except in the case of brief quotations embodied in critical reviews and certain other noncommercial uses permitted by copyright law.

Names, characters, events, and incidents are the products of the author's imagination. Any resemblance to actual persons, living or dead, or actual events is purely coincidental.

humans are the only species known to blush.

she is going
to be
someone who is
folk music
a better basketball player

                                                               rebellious.

table of contents

THE BARDS AND THE BEES 1

WHET 23

ROSY OUTLOOKS 77

STOP AND SMELL THE ROSES 99

ACKNOWLEDGEMENTS 161

ABOUT THE AUTHOR 163

Rosy-Cheeked

the bards and
the bees

Rosy-Cheeked

rosy-cheeked

I ask mom:
where's dad?
what's my lineage?

she says:
you're a half-burned rubber NASCAR track
full of leaving
and always asking
to come back.
you're all
green-light-and-gas-pedal *go*.
you are part
short fuse
and starting over
with another family.
you are birth-marked
in cigarettes
and Bud Light.
you are brunette
just like him.

darling,
your flesh
and future
are all rose.
but
you are generational trauma.
even though there's incest
in our ancestry
there's so much

more to our history
I'd like to remember.
I'm doing my
best to lead you through this
alone.

you are a lot of what
he made you
to be
I am afraid
to say.
you're daring
and delinquent.
quiet rage.
furled fist.
ready to swing.
a fuse
scared of its own spark.
you are always right
(even when you're wrong).
you are throwing away
instructions for life.

I am afraid
to say
to you
that you
are part
illusionist—
never showing
the world
you share
his same
suffering.

Rosy-Cheeked

you are handcuffed steel
holding yourself back
from the cell.

but
my dear
rosy-cheeked girl,
you are no line up.
you are no age of death.
you are the lineage you choose.

but most of all,
you've got
my bankrupt blue eyes,
honey,
I hope that amounts to something.
I've been penny-pinching.
here's a piggy bank—
let's piggy back
on a plan.

the state can't get him to pay
court-ordered child support
but we've got spaghetti
on the table tonight.
meatballs, too.
mangia, mangia.

all my old haunts

a high-school basketball court
hardwood floors
a hollow spot
by the three-point line
hung-up jerseys
hallmarking the ghosts
of alumni bygone.

the greasy-palmed Century 16 theater
seating ourselves in red-velvet
the R-rated horrors we snuck into
on a triple dog dare.

a downtown 1800s cemetery
collecting names off granite cobwebbed headstones
to give to my computer-game Sims characters.

the neighborhood plant nursery's pumpkin patch
my sister selecting an autumn's gold
to gut in Halloween's scare.
me—
refusing to carve into the past.

grownups
understand only
in the passage of calendars
how long childhood lasts.

We hopscotch through a clock—
*how many skips does it
take to encircle the house?*
162.

Exhale dandelions
bubble-blowing
constellations of daylight.
Picnic-blanket bustle
PB&J jokers
otter
POP, the kiddie pool.
Hula
(basketball) hoop
BOUNCE
on trampoline time.
Zinc nose
grass siesta—
s'more of the dog days, please.

Each summer I would tell my mother:
Slugs travel at the speed of sidewalk.

bed-wetter chronicles

Shhhhhh.
Don't trust your dreams,
the piss-poor potty trainer warned.
They're tricksters.

When I was in elementary school,
I went to bed-wetting class.

"Accidents" were frequent—
sleepovers, relatives' couches, cots,
anywhere but home.
My body betrayed me
in the most efficient way:
pee while asleep.
Kill two birds,
one warm puddle.

So my mom hired a "consultant."
I called him the "piss-poor trainer."
He installed a high-tech vinyl mat
beneath my sheets,
which was wired to an alarm box.
That box—a beast.
At the first drop of liquid,
it howled.
The objective? Simple:
Teach me to stop wetting,
or should I say
"whetmanning,"
the bed.

Rosy-Cheeked

Every night,

when liquid met mat,

the machine would erupt—

a shriek, a snarl,

an electronic banshee.

It yanked me from dreams

into a fluorescent reality.

The new ritual:

Bed.
Alarm.
Bathroom.
Back to bed.

At first, I'd just lie there—

wet-bottomed and content.

Dreaming of toilets.

Vivid. White. Plentiful.

So. Many. Toilets.

My mind, the saboteur,

whispered:

you're safe.

pee here.

let it flow, baby.

The golden drizzle.

A twin bed turned porcelain throne.

Retrospe(e)ctively,
I'm not sure how long it took me to stop
wetting the bed.

(Maybe I just outgrew it?)
But even now,

sometimes,
I still dream

I am floating
       d
             o
                  w
                       n
                               stream

on a river

of golden toilets.

Australia bans kids from social media

and I think back
to being a kid in the 90s:
the cellphone-less era.

Our bodies swung bar to bar,
little monkeys in playground motion.
We bedazzled our shirts,
our backpacks,
our imaginations—
not buried in the blue light of screens,
but lit up by *The Wizard of Oz*.

We weren't scrolling.
We were flipping through *Highlights*,
dog-earing pages of *National Geographic for Kids*.
"Text" meant books—
the ones on our summer reading lists,
cracked spines and library due dates.

Sure, we had video games,
but car rides weren't for *Candy Crush*.
They were for the License Plate Game,
for catching clues bumper by bumper,
for *20 Questions*
and asking:
Would you rather grow up now or **back then**?

We didn't spot cell towers—
just power lines.
We ganged up on A to Z
in the Alphabet Game.
C? No cell phone.
I? No Instagram.

Just Punch Buggy!
No punch back.
Shoulders bruised.
Backseat warriors.

We played the Quiet Game
before social media told us to be silent.
We named names:
Shel Silverstein
Naomi Shihab Nye
Emily Dickinson
Natalie Diaz.

Never Have I Ever
been so disconnected
by what's meant to connect us.

Social media—
causing more than just
Six Degrees of Separation.

daddy don't

say a slurred-word
sorry. don't slam
a door then glug
your seventh Budweiser.

Daddy, don't
believe beer-bottle comfort
replaces family.

Daddy, don't
make me watch
a porno film
at 10
don't teach me
love is only
(un)dressed flesh.
don't make female
objectification
your motto.

Daddy, don't.
Don't testify that strength
is sanctimonious.
don't make a bible
out of black eyes.

Daddy, don't
teach me
how to drive
with boozy breath

bloodshot eyes
watering behind the wheel
don't tell the officer
don't DUI
with me in the back
again…

don't
tell me you're wearing cologne
to the daddy daughter dance.
I know the scent of an alcoholic.

Daddy, don't
embarrass me.
The neighbors are whispering
from their windows
as law enforcement knocks
on our front door
again (domestic disturbance)
and
again (wellness check)
and
again (assault).

Daddy, don't
make me cry.
I hide
in the closet
holding cloth for comfort.

Arguments last
days
weeks
months

years.

Daddy, don't
yell at me.
Defensive rebuttals
are no reason
for drunken punishment.

Daddy, don't
take off your belt.
How wicked to want
submission.
To want pleasure
from my pain.
Tears fall
faster than whip.

Daddy, don't.
You are merely a stranger
now. Daddy,
allow me...
to forget
you. Daddy...
*How could someone
like you
create someone
like me?*

Daddy,
don't look at me...
because I fear
one day
I will see myself.

one-liner memoirs

Learning freedom with clipped wings

Popcorn, poetry, pickup lines, pastimes.

Trading in one court for another.

Contingent-She: Playing through every scenario.

The price is right

Encircled by a chain-link fence
in a browning backyard
I etched an *S.O.S.* in the dirt.
Only one way out (and in).
My day-time keeper:
a woman named Shirley.
She was short-haired;
short-tempered.
I plucked earthen stems
and blew seedy wishes
into the wind.
Waited.

Popcorn ceilings
plastic-wrapped sofas
a speck of a child
she dusted off
each wood-legged piece
on a keeping-up-with-the-Joneses **payment plan:**
"Cataloged comforts."
My mother, too, indebted in a way.
My care: paid by mom's piggy-bank savings.

How did I occupy the rigid hours, you ask?
I built towers of Babel
out of Beanie Babies
made ships succumb
to toilet whirlpools.
I *reached*
for the sky and

for my *Toy Story* Woody doll,
for the top-shelf Cheetos bag.
The Price is Right reruns
on Channel 2 static.
Chainsmoke filtering in
through a half-opened window.
That game-show childhood
Bob Barker bellowed:
Come on down!
You're the next contestant....
I ran closer to the screen:
I guessed the price
of a clutch of twelve:
$1.75.

By afternoon,
I would dislodge myself
from a sunken couch cushion
when the deadbolt door peeled
open. There was mom—
freshly clocked out.
A maternal greeting:
Let's go get ice cream!
An end-of–a-shift
ice-cream cone—
creamy therapy.
Mom was a sweet-treat fairy
when she knew fury awaited
back at home
on Haven Street
where our "family" was reclusive.
Empty-table evenings
echos of a drunkard
Mom's lips stained

like red spaghetti
again: leftovers of a fist.
Go-to-bed-early commands
late nights with nicotine
for dad. Mom cried
over spilled milk
unpaid bills.
Eviction edict
tacked to the
window(pain).
Luck and lactose—
Mom: intolerant
to both.

The next day
we left
penniless
that house
(and him).
Suitcase
sister
mom driving the
near-full-tank sedan
away. Dandelion hands
letting go like a Plinko
puck, parachute-less
not fully knowing
where
to
land.

My mother was 30
when we left him—
the age I am now

while I am
writing this.
I have a dozen
yolk-filled ovals
in hand.
I return
to his Haven:
a shelling
of cracked white
sieges memory lane.

A carton of eggs
now costs
$2.34.

gifts you can't wrap

My mom is the best gift-giver I've ever known. This isn't a matter of opinion—it's fact. In third grade, "Santa" brought me a basketball hoop. I became a collegiate basketball player.

In eighth grade, she gave me a luggage set. She knew I was going places. Two decades later, the same closest-on-wheels accompanies me when I travel.

But some gifts can't be wrapped.

Like the memory of my great-grandfather—a true family man—serving spaghetti to his great-grandchildren, singing *When the moon hits your eye like a big pizza pie, that's amoreeeeee.*

Or our backyard bocce ball tournaments—overly competitive. Or seeing him in the stands at every basketball game until my freshman year of college. That season, after a late shift at my part-time job, I got the call: It was time.

I drove 20 minutes in silence to his house. There he was—catatonic in his worn green chair; the Utah Jazz flickering on ESPN static, just celebrating a victory. My great-grandfather was a Stockton-to-Malone loyalist, a survivor of seven heart attacks, and on that December night, just before Christmas, he passed. Peacefully. Watching *his* team.

The gift I'll never forget came days later.

At our annual family Christmas gathering, something was missing. Grandpa Johnny's chair was empty. We opened presents. We said *thanks*. But nothing felt like enough—not in the absence of Grandpa Johnny.

Then my mom stood up. "Wait," she said. "I've got one more." She left the room, returned with a box for each great-grandchild—Build-a-Bear boxes, tiered and unmistakable.

We opened them. Stuffed bears dressed like each of us down to our style and quirks. And then—silence. Until we heard it.

Each bear spoke. Not with a factory voice, but with his. There, my great-grandfather's voice, preserved inside each bear. A personalized message for each of us. *Lancee, keep on shooting. Mangia mangia. I love you.*

Gifts. Some come with bows. Others are unwrappable. My mother, with that present, gave us time—a memory to hold, a voice to remember, a moment that made us all fall quiet. The best gifts often leave you speechless.

Rosy-Cheeked

whet

Rosy-Cheeked

bottled up

The absence of feeling reeling inside;
I surmise,
by emotions un-rectified.

missed meteorite

Warp-speed ceiling-fan stare down. Dead-space
bed. Alien-form depression. UFO inconvenience.

A friend asks: *What's your outlook on life?*
I respond: *I am a lonely meteorite.*

Crashing, burning, other-life-form brain occupation.
My spewing will make more sense one day.

For now, my earthen self is sassy, salty, shit-faced,
sad. Outer-world experience.

Aspirations to launch. I want to be stationed
elsewhere. Halley's Comet of hyphenated phrases.

Hubble Telescope and Helvetica font. *Help,*
send more help. Punctuation marks—

my only gravity. No astronomy, just distressed
sentences to stardust. I have this

space-time continuum life—
a black hole for a heart.

runway

Pray to the airport gods for jet-stream grace.
Each insecurity gets a pat-down
by a stranger's hands.
Random selection feels less
random lately—
more probing,
more personal.
A passenger of unfamiliarity,
I drift.
Runways harbor too many **runaways**.
There's purgatory—
and then there's this place.
Almost on equal planes.
Gravity isn't done with me.
It has more weight to give
before takeoff;
before the motion sickness.
The sky feels surreal
when I finally give it
my undivided attention.
Attention. Attention.
17D begins descent.
Deep-blue views of the Pacific.
A final warning from each attendant.
I know:
only angels
are well practiced
at flight.
Still—perhaps,
just perhaps—

there's a promise.
That somewhere above 10,000 feet,
I'll find peace.

all things ephemeral

Hay-bale arms—
I'm a straw woman.
Leapfrog words,
say everything but the jaded truth.

Sweet-and-sticky life,
honey outlooks,
crabapple personality,
top-branch aspirations.

Shooting-star runaway,
fading like a promise.
Lighthouse eyes guide
me to flow states,
grin as big as a bride's bouquet.

Dirt roads, a staple—
low on stock, low on spirit.
Salt-lick lips,
staring down fence posts.

Into bondage, but
not boundary-setting.
Flirt me into foreplay,
mend the atmosphere.
The price of pumpernickel satiation,
meditation a meager sacrifice.

Artificial anxiety,
antidepressant artery.

Ache for longevity,
short-term girl.

Is trust a normality?

Sun numb, night runs.
Escapism—just a delay tactic.
Last-time aridity.

All I am
is a side effect of water.

Rosy-Cheeked

doing of

My sister asks: *How are you?*
I reply: *When have I ever been well?*
Wellbutrin's got me down
And the downers have got me up.
It's backwards,
My thinking,
And my shirt
And my shit
That I step in
Each morning
Because I forget
To clean
Up
My own damn mess.

Bathroom Break

thin-ply people pleaser
a performance: sponsored by Prozac.
rocket-science life,
graduate-degree decongestant—
pedigree…
is the dog food I purchase.
I read the in(de)structions
black-coffee tired
bad-posture reflection
I play the victim of a desk job
I play the hero of paper jams
fiber
optic cable installations
low on broccoli
and snail mail
smuggling
yellow-brick-road trauma
to therapy.
I only see the wizard
on weed and Wagnalls,
~~Funk.~~ *fuck.*
God, I need help.
there is no damn plunger.

Anti-*liability*-depressant

Anti: opposed to; against.
Depressant: reducing functional or nervous activity.

I took the pill
and swallowed water.

Befriend my brain.

I bite
my nails.
Cuticular strength.

It's refilled.
The prescription—
not the glass
I flush
my system with.

The pill, wallows.
Wellbutrin gallows.

It's the sun that burns
the most, I say.
They diagnose the shade.

I take the pill
and swallow water.

Insurance. Liability.
Suture a smile.

*Let's talk about
what happened*, inquiries
from Someone therapeutic,
charting retrogression.

Water, gurgles.
It's a hurdle
to hold milligrams.

The self portrait
of sad science
with sharp cutlery.
Crimson belongs best
to lips and lovers—
not the languishing artery.

I took that pill
and swallowed the water.

It's costly,
I know
to confuse
coffin
with
living.
Reincarnate relief.

Numbness of a heart.
Induction of a bridge.
When you say: *Jump!*
I say: *How high?*

One last time
I swallow

Rosy-Cheeked

only water.

8

I am a latecomer to life. Idle
remembrance of the womb. Anatomical

name, rolling in like fog, like
fumigation, like suffocation. I just

wish the world wasn't so
sanctimonious when it teaches me

another hard-fought lesson. Too many
wounds treated with rubbed-in dirt. Abandoned

by the days; the bleeding-heart bulb
senescing in late summer. With paths

set in stone, I saunter down recurring
loops. Traveling in figure eights

makes the journey all the more
infinite.

Rosy-Cheeked

*metal stability—
in this economy?*

serving up sertraline
milligrams: my favorite appetizer

                       meatball pills, *am I (full) enough?*
                       so not al dente, this depression.

long-noodle nonsense
nodes of phlegm fortitude

                       napkin-stained crimson
                       counting my macro-

carbohydrate economics
supply of spaghetti veins

                       demanding a diagnosis
                       carb (un)loading on my friends

lost in the **sauce of life:**
a jar of **marinara**

costs less   than therapy.

extra! extra!

Maybe

people

tend

to forget

us

the way

we

forget

yesterday's

headlines.

drain

How fragile is forgiveness?
What about relapse?

It's easier to pardon what others do to us
than what we do to ourselves.

Spilled wine on wishful thinking—
stained outlooks,
overclocked brain,
short-circuiting sins.

It looks different for each of us.
Stuck inside worn exoskeletons,
until we molt or melt—
either way,
transformation is coming.

Practiced mirror goodbyes.
Let it crack
at the sight
of freckled indecision.

Stilled fragments,
broken reflection free-
fall.

Glass cuts the aftermath.
Sinew shatters, too.

A million bathroom affirmations

don't change us like they promise.

Grip a calloused doorknob
for false anchorship.

Unload a stomach
into porcelain.
Throw-up throne.
Queen of knees.
Bathroom disciple.
Linoleum pew.
Purge unkept promises—
I need to be flushed
out of my own system;
floored
by my own submission.
What's emptied
is everlasting.

Tears—so buoyant,
I float.
Life-vest vestiges.

When things go down
the drain,
I still find it so silly,
the way water

s
    w
  i
      r
        l
s.

nine one one

Yoke the alarm clock
into another modality.
Time   s   p   l   i   c   e   s
at each second's backbone.
Call the operator.
Nine, one, one.
One, two, three—
you counted.
The bridge—
just another backdrop.
Stance,
a support system so unwilling.
You always said
you were *Captain of the Atlantic.*
The deep

had other plans

to take

your eyes

gave themselves
to the sea.
I held your mother's hands
like
                      b u o y.
I'm not one for reruns.
Reruns. Not one
to replay the scene

where you
befriended
the sky.

Rosy-Cheeked

sun block

I may be sentient
but I still block

the sun. sometimes
I have an arsenal

of odd reactions
to light; semi-formal relapse

into your radiating arms.
it's a burning displacement

of myself. I mutter
my fiery name. if only

I could
remember it.

would you stand through this shit & make it out?

you would / paint over the swear-word graffiti / the rusted outline of decay / the iron from your steel-toed boots / stalling alloy from afterlife / you would be / an artist / you would

sink each Barbie doll / how could you / play God / play makeover / with wet hair / dunked on epiphany / the way childhood is devoured / with plastic / & pink / a throwaway age / that was only advertised in film / & infomercial hope / to rid me of problem / & psoriasis / yet

adulting is an Adirondack chair / laid back ambivalence / i look like / a northeastern squall / in the Target / home goods aisle / no place to put a mirror / for waterproof mascara / & teary applications

i know / the first reason / for **tight shoe laces / & socks** / is to withstand / the cold.

solar eclipse

I'm all imposter. I want to tell
a lie just to hear it. It's

a syndrome. There are nothing
but swear words in my sailor's

mouth. Under this silver-armored neck-
lace are chest-plated platitudes. Often,

I see how others turn away
from me like the ignorance

of the change clingers on I-90.
I may be stepping into a puddle

of piss or leftover spray paint:
a half-assed attempt

at graffiti—concreteness
or correctness?

I want to die
young. Twenty-nine

lives. I start
believing the tarot cards,

The Fool. Folks, like me,
sit on bridges,

taking pleasure in the looking
down. The water blackens,

eclipsed by the sun,
momentarily. Just enough

to know I am burning more
brain than choroid. Confused

corneas. Spectating
at this skyward part

of the simulation. Dodged
daylight and the drunken

stupor. The future's pretty
foolproof, I guess. I'll slip

into a necktie
or noose

little nuances
in nouns.

What's the difference? Tell
me. In one ear and out

the other. Childhood
tendencies. I can't stop thinking

about the end. Wholly
and indefinitely. Eternal

and inconsequential. All I can do

Rosy-Cheeked

is squint

my eyes. Will I ever be
more human

than a half-crescent
host?

Lancee Whetman

Burn notice

Mornings are so unremitting
(most days).
I greet the door
with slackened hand,

off to only God knows
where—
my day job).

(likely
The hours decide
what I do
(or don't).

It's the Monday
waltz again,
dancing to society's tempo.

Life is
too inviolable
to ignore.

To spark belief,
I carry a pack of cheap matches.
That should do the trick.

No wick needed;
enough.
I'm flammable
too many stories
I've heard
about ash.
about rising;
front desk.
Phoenix of the
Paperweight stories—

Rosy-Cheeked

call it
organizational   restructuring.
I nominate myself
for a directorship.
An office   edict
from a new
chain of command.
It burns—
this sensation   of remembering how
to live.
Under fluorescent lights,
                                                      I leave behind

a waxen trace,
unscented
but unmistakable.
This candle
blazes   a beginning.
I say *hello*
                                                   to my new self,

leaving the arsonist
behind.

steam bath

Logically,
the wine doesn't mix

well with the antidepressants.
Steaming out

the toxins, purge nirvana
through sweat. Exorcise

mind with eucalyptus.
Accept the shape of shadow.

Tolerate the flickers
of light. Body—

a storage unit
for excess

water—a happenstance
of chaos. Still,

transition into
treasure, I glisten,

 albeit
momentarily.

if function

if you call,
another heartbreak poem
        follows
causation, undoubtedly.

pitchin'
                a
                            fit
closed-mouthed.
clothes on.
closer
to contingency.
i
to letter
u.

if warm handprints
wear me
thin…

I will let them:
tension the surface
compromise a Thursday
falsify my body
equate at horizontal.

if…
habits are not
happenstance
confuse

            the two.

unnoticeable
when a mirror
                                                            reflects.

                        who are we
                        when we aren't
                        in error?

instigate your imprint
bludgeon the (bed)sheet
induce a tear.

I find myself
most often
in the *farewell*
never negating
the locket
of a liar.

even though *this*
then *that*—
if functions
excel at
irrationality.

like, for example,
after *goodbye,*
if you call,
I'll still say *hello.*
still,
despite this,
as much

Rosy-Cheeked

as I want to,
I'll never
cast aspersions
to your name.

you will heal (in time)

Too many folks are
patience-is-a-virtue preachers.
You'll get over it soon.
Their sentinel sentiments
irk me like flat beer.

It's in my nature to give
second chances to an ex's
unconscionability.

Call me
out like bullshit
card games
like strike
threes.

I give grace
to each alarm clock
snooze.

By 7 a.m., I have pardoned
all the glances he gave me
back then;
back when he was
the reason for each cellular

Rosy-Cheeked

e   x   l   s   i   o
           p   o   n

I gave the butterflies
an early retirement
by 8 a.m.

Let the tool finally rust
by 10 a.m.

Being as in love
and as
indefinite
as the

        w
                i   d
                      n

is my greatest achievement.

spiraling 2.0

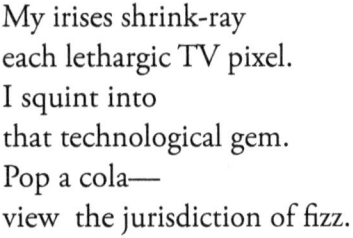

Send correspondence to hell.
To: the Devil
Subject: Heel.

Scars from the sin
of the sofa
are surely defeating.
The carpet feels more
cast iron
than soft
condolence.

My irises shrink-ray
each lethargic TV pixel.
I squint into
that technological gem.
Pop a cola—
view the jurisdiction of fizz.

Each morning,
I take a freight train
of potassium;.
life is a construction site.

Sunburns: a midsummer perk.
Frostbite: the cost of doing business
with winter.
History is a feudalism scalawag.
I fiddle with premonitions,
fault myself for having

Rosy-Cheeked

too much

v
o
l
u
m
e.

Growing up means I'm kin
to agriculture.
Genetics deserve a round
of applause—
maybe some applesauce, too.
Do I have a standing-ovation purpose?
My grave needs reformation
before I repose
in familiar craters.
Chrysalis, my sin.
Zen, my scythe.

Payments now go toward
forgotten passwords.
There's a throb
in reimbursing mistakes.

I am a foster-child riddle.
The elms must listen
to the crimes
of Christmas carolers.
Serve them zigzag bark
'n wrap it like a candy cane.

Each light-year thrill

is rotational insanity.
I purge the magnetism
of virtuosity.

Hip-check the stop sign
so I miss the household turn-
pike.
Every rut
along the way
is a cure.

Rosy-Cheeked

proof of sanity

is bushwhacking through paisley patterns / sprinting through a downpour of forget-me-nots / taking your shadow self to couples therapy / x-ray-ing your peanut butter and jelly sandwiches / bombing all your bathtubs with epsom salt / drawing a colorless rainbow / kissing a bumblebee / not being aware of the sting.

incoherence

The glance is an unrequited equation.

We are pressed for time
like sandwich marketing.

Becoming senior is a slow

g
r
a
d
i
e
n
t.

Realism, an unknown achievement.

Give me a slab of a country
that I would recognize.

nightmares

Open-water swimming; shark-shadow insanity. Rooftop stumble; heart-in-throat thrill. Sky-scraper jump; free-fall dread. Childhood-home ghosts; dead remembrance. Full-priced shopping; wallet-ache insomnia. Hot-wired adrenaline; joy-ride suspense. Cliff-edge dive; limb dismemberment. Crystal ball fate; psychic predicaments. Tarot-card contrition; unveiled future. He tells his mother he loves me; a secret unjailed.

no meaning in text messages

Lobby a response.
Lancee can no longer be reached.

The only meaning I find now is in an F-flat. The piano is in shambles—or maybe that's just a metaphor for the person playing it. I find virtue in not being good at difficult things: neuroscience, calculus, replying to text messages. I want, so badly, to set down every line of communication open to me. Lobby a cell-phone company. Survey the reach, the geography of snail mail. Portugal, Ireland, as far as wind-chime bells. I'll write something as affecting as Beethoven's *Moonlight Sonata*.

F-flat.
Shambled pianist.
Being bad. Being good.
There's an indiscriminate virtue in both.
Calculate the benefits
of snail-mail communication.
Portugal is a windchime.
Moonlight Sonata—another geography.

Rosy-Cheeked

waking up and hating it

comatose in a REM cycle / & horizontal ache / like the midnight sheep counters / I cover up / in the antagonistic properties of silk /

the light is diffused / forces awakening / a slight twitch / at the duty of rising / like memory vertigo / vertical spinal / chord / of a vertebrae crack / coffee verdicts / it's the unpredicted violations of rest / relapse to a sheet.

the alarm stutters / an inhale of an eyelash / it is this moment / monotony / of being /

alive & yet wishing / you were exempt from the task.

don't read the eulogy yet

The past has become

                more assertive than usual;
                        it's unfair to be

disciplined
in forgetting.

Jealousy can be

                        so avant-garde;

unaware
of the

                compare-then-collapse

hypothesis.

Gloom floats

                in uneven distributions

over my left temple;
as if remembering

                the needle-therapy illusion

The park fence thaws,

                    heaves a little less;

there's a sunrise now—
nearly

                          shouting.

I know there are other ways
to feel

Rosy-Cheeked

the free fall.
I know I don't want

to come too early.

a stranger's *welcome*
can be rehabilitative

the floating,

a eulogy

I know that

if you let it.

I can't find my nail clippers

and now—the whole world is ending.
I only wanted simple self-care, not a spiral.
But here it comes again—
the breakdown, weekly as a Sunday sermon.

Backsliding to the bathroom floor,
the tile cradles what I can't—
what I haven't been able to.

I check the weight of my heart on the scale,
stopped measuring how large a soul can swell.

I hoped the wishes I tossed
in that downtown fountain as a kid
would've bloomed by now—

the want for first light,
to be fast asleep.

Blackjack tongue, tasting Vegas asphalt—
I want juniper,
jumping jacks above the tree line,
the will to live.

Willow vows, wood-stove partnership,
songs meant for record players—
caulking an open wound with a chord,

Rosy-Cheeked

the decadence of harmonica static.

I want hands sifting the sands of time,
dogs shaking off the day's dandruff.

I want dirty nails.
Nothing to trim.

helpless

Put me on the counter.
Butcher-block fate.
Count each cutlery wound.

Expectation is a non-existent chorus.
Ring around the nosy
demons, games—
this playground
personhood.

Fumble another disposable life.
Ruin the arterial film—
all unprocessed memory fluid.

Snap shot the stratosphere.
Click click incandescence.

Give a smile.
Say *sorry*.
Wear it forever.

Press a button.
Pull a trigger.
It's the same motion
that stops time.

unstable poem

Hydroplane down the same Main Street—
lost my job, my man, my sanity.

They say the belly of the beast
is where gold is forged.
But I want mountain peaks,
not to keep playing in the gorge.

Catholic school said: *Pray to the Lord.*
I don't understand angelic verse,
only corrupt chords.

Time trickles by like the bathroom sink.
I've got justice in my heart,
but the law shakes at the knees.

Can't catch a break,
can't meet a deadline.
Is responsibility my fate,
or fated by design?

I give my days for a damned salary.
Was told false sweet-nothing flattery.

I don't know how to play,
but I'll pluck a string,
sing about being rich—
what they call "stability."

Is there a pill I could take,

a place I could go?
Why do I chase
the places that are all unknown?

Take me back,
take me back
to those northern skies—
limitless reach,
where your breath matched mine.

Now I'm all alone,
in a state where desert meets dust.
Is this where I'll meet my maker,
where I'll finally rust?

the moon is no good

Defend the darkness.
Skim the gas pedal.
"Gone" is the only real emergency.
Transitions are my friends,
but they are dramatic racehorses.
Sherbet tastes like sincere youth.
It is poor judgment to predict
when you'll ever be "ready."

I suppose my poor judgment is beneficial—morsel comprehension, howling at the thirteenth, biting at Friday. I can be sincere as sherbet: melted-tongue communicant. Ready as a racehorse, too. They tell me to be more coyote in my trite wonder, to stop being dramatic. I ask: Have you told this to the moon? Ubiquitous transitions make me far from tranquil this waning crescent. Control is a claustrophobic friend with her gas-pedal emergencies. Set my location to "gone." Skim the darkness off my degeneracy. Spike the serendipity with a touch of spite. Blame mood swings on Mercury as defense. Hark in a synonym for a sound truth: it'll all be real and resolute eventually.

Comprehend coyotes.
Wonder is ubiquitous;
I find it in moon-shades.
Claustrophobic emergency.
Serendipity degenerate.
I spike my synonyms;
am resolute about Mercury.

paying the bills

Fever-pitch prodding. I'm part of the cattle crowd, rich in shit-stepping. Fancy-restaurant guilt. Unfooled, yet furled, by minimum wage. I can't wait to bottle up the pennies—how much are they worth now, in their decommissioned state?

Poetry is the only escape I can afford. Alcohol is disadvantaged therapy. Spirit guides, dote on me: confidence. Can I bend my mind, all downward-dog diction?

I go to the gym to be more mentally acute—longevity legs, brain-goop muscles. Hard work will give me open-road freedom, a whipped-hair, rolled-down-window, desert-sunshine aesthetic.

Is part of perfecting my craft the sharing of it? Is it moral bargaining to deprive ourselves of destiny? I pledge my words as a soul-level offering.

I am forthcoming frustration. Dipped, partially, in acrylic abundance. The other half, dismal as a **warring dime**.

my master, the too-dark

Earth hope.
Ego preheated.
Awe-stricken
by the knotted cottonwoods,
the cattails.
Confess that
the essence
of being present
means I am
coming
to terms
with being
less.

This bird-winged hope. I look back on the past, too far into the future, forget that my fists are for the present. Confess that the smoke that I've raised was awe-stricken grief. Dismiss the lesser-black backed gull for well, being lesser. Isn't that how it goes? If something is labeled, that must be its essence? Philosophical much? Poetic not? Knot the references to hurled cottonwood. The cattails, I find, are all pointing West. My master is the too-dark. Pistols go to temples, my temple. One word, interpret the meaning. Either way, the heaping of a heart takes place. Outcomes are stark, but it's almost changing time. What does that entail? A coming-to-terms? With what? Preheated Earth? Predestined egos?

It's too dark not to know
the philosophy of pistols,
the temple of the poet—
talk about
the heapings of labels.
How one is dismissed
as "lesser."
Interpret my
essence,
my fisted outcomes.

Rosy-Cheeked *phoenix*

When you see a rose,
do you reconcile my cheeks
pressed to yours?
As if color still held resonance
like daybreak on yellow sheet?

Back when love was still
a simple phenomenon,
a prism-rainbow pleasure.
It was enough to just exist
in light.
No need for much tending—
just touch,
a little water,
a bit of walking,
like the dog.

I excavate an ending,
slowly close the curtains on chapters.
Sell the flour, the flower.
How? Her?
Pursuit has its thrill,
but ego is
your fiercest opponent.

Now, our bodies crave
more centrifugal force
to get us moving
out of bed,
and into ourselves again.

It's time you tell me
one last story, old lover.
Tell me about the Phoenix.
Would you ever admit it
if you were the one
who set her on fire?

body dysmorphia

the mirror lies
when it tells me
I have concavity-cratered pores—
blemished biology
bombarding my face.

the mirror lies
when it reflects
an obese organism
a belle of the ball
a curvaceous creature
a starved skeleton
athleticism's bulge
anorexia's snack
mental health scars
just-right skin.

Is this house-of-mirrors misinformation
or mixed-mirror magic?

dear Prudence

Now, I'm not one for blasting my sexuality across the seam of the internet—
but God forbid a thread gets frayed.
And here we are: three horizontal stripes deep.

Privilege looks a lot like passing.
Passing looks a lot like not being gay.
My hair's never been short, my Carhartt never obvious enough,
my swagger never mistaken for something other than straight.

Still, I've been known to get giddy over nail-polished niceties,
highlighted hair hellos,
but also being held by a buckskin hunting coat in a Ram 2500.
It's the indecision of pursuing gender,
the flavor-flipping, the soft contradictions of choice.
The people I find intriguing cross lines
while I look the part—
straight (or at least passing).

When I first moved to Alaska, they'd always ask,
Did you come up with your husband?
When I go play pickup basketball,
I get asked if my boyfriend plays, too.
It looks like getting bought a drink by the man across the bar
while your short-haired butch friend gets her car keyed
for, well—
for having short hair,
for looking like a label lesbian.

Rosy-Cheeked

At the club, my rainbow friends
do the dirty work.
I still get to dance silly
while they suffer
the effects of a slur.

What's the impropriety of being gay?
Is it in the gestures, the glances, the gait?
I pass like flying colors—pink, purple, blue.
But I don't block a butch who calls it what it is: privilege.

Privilege isn't an equation.
Being queer isn't a competition.
If you're out, you can be proud—
but bi pride demands, at least,
passing recognition if you have it,
protecting those without it.

I don't have more to say than this:
The world still judges book covers.
And mine, I know,
is less likely to be burned
than hers.

dna

My body knows
>no different. Go up
>>the DNA staircase. Look
>in the ATGC attic.

My body knows
>genetics.
>>It knows recessiveness,
eczema,
excessive sweat.
>My body knows
>>tear ducts,
>toenails,
tongue-twisted
>talking.
>>It knows
>two left feet,
faltering.
>It knew
>>peanuts.
>It knows
epinephrine.
>My body is
>>biology:
>all brain—
no beauty.
>It knows
>>moon cycles
>cramps
motor control
>hypothalamus hunger.

Rosy-Cheeked

        But my body
    silences
serotonin;
    does not
        know a damn
    depressive
difference.
    My body
        once
    knew
this name.

grin
and bear those bad genetics.
Fourth incisor from the front:
previously gapped.
A wire-tightened repair
colloquially known as a "brace face."
Whistling capabilities be gone!
Fuck me up in the floss
gums a-bleeding.
A second failed root canal
an extraction—
cause for concern or a crown?
Implant a molar
sedate me with laughing gas.
I've had my fair share of fillings—
another cavity on canine #11.
Sharpened vampirical evidence
savagely tearing away
at my meaty male meals
in iron devour.
An underbite.
Help-me-out headgear;
I'm an elastic-banded beauty.
Fixing the face
of my fifteen-year old self.
Rinse
and
repeat.
Gagged by grape-flavored fluoride.
A grin
a gargle

Rosy-Cheeked

a gingivitis giggle.
An ode
to the overly enthusiastic orthodontist
the oracular oral surgeon.
A dedication
to my die-hard dentist.
I'll keep them on retainer
because my mother
didn't spend all that money
for me not to smile
(even if it's fake).

ayurvedic acne

sebum is an oil that helps keep skin from drying out.
the overproduction of it, however, clogs pores.

the result: nefarious acne.
blackhead
whitehead
no-discrimination pimples.

put puberty aside, I am an adult now.
heredity
stress
what have you,
I want clear skin,
naturally,
I swap
the oil-based makeup
the harsh soap
the frenzied scrubbing
for
chick-pea paste face masks (made from scratch)
cumin, coriander, and fennel tea (organic)
turmeric and sandalwood face cream (ayurvedic, of course).

zonk a zit with
evening primrose oil
black currant oil
tea-tree oil treatments.
oy vey!

Resorting to a Dr. Bronner's soap bar,

Rosy-Cheeked

I tell my face:
please, act your age.

butch

low-ceilinged smiles rule the morning
black coffee kind-of-good.
on the front stoop,
she looks at the world with
pride. eyes
like a scythe,
girlish (at times).
she isn't
what a woman
is told to be.
when she wants,
she wears
her dad's XXXL t-shirt,
disguised by defensive Raiders cotton,
& baggy Nike polyester.
she is
tight-end tender,
quiffed-hair charisma,
the do-it-yourself daughter.
she is
blade &
battlefield.
some would even say
beautiful.

the big girl

Stretch extra-large
measurements.

Hunger for skinny
dip.

Disappear
into the just-out-of-the-shower
mirror fog.

Ignore the reflection—
the repulsion.

Always
a two-for-one seat
a supersize meal
a scale error.

Why is my only hope
to shrink?

one piece, two piece

Interrupt a sand dune to
talk about drifting
plots of memory.

Beach-towel tired—
what is in between our toes
is out of reach
gritty.

Silence
the seashells
in my ear.

Old-man wind
wants to devour
a surfer, riding a sunburn
high.

Wave
down a life
guard.

The rain-
bowed umbrella
is a shady lance.

My swimsuit, garnish
to skin.

pride

I charter the sidewalk cracks
for sure steps
right directions.

I despise "or" ultimatums.
Desire the "and."
And, so be it.
And, this is
me.
And I am
proud to say
it.

Give me
a cornucopia
of constructive comments,
pronouns that precede
acceptance.

I don't want Louis Vuitton
progress.
Give me thrifted change
so queer & stylish
everyone can afford
to wear it.

Don't hand me hope
stitched together
with "if,"
"but,"

or "maybe."

But, I am patient.
But, I am waiting.
But, I am
this.

I am firework
loud.
Celebration worthy.

And, I want a nation
as bold as a parade float,
waving rainbow flags,
and embracing
every letter
of the aLpHaBeT.

COVID or hard water made my hair fall out

The day
of the every-three-months hair trim,
the hairdresser inquires:
When did you decide to get layers?
Tears swell
in the swivel chair
and she inspects
the choppy
uneven lengths—
loss from something
against volition.
Conglomerates of hair balls
were commingling
in my bathroom,
refraining from staying
in their rightful pore.
Patchy isn't posh.
*Perhaps it was the aftermath
of my COVID stint
or the hard water
in the town in which I live?*
In her short-hair demure,
she speaks
of her cancer-survival story—

the true pain
of women's attachment
to their scalps.
She says:
Your hair will grow back.
It is growing back.
Mine, too.

Rosy-Cheeked *crayon*

I dare you
to embrace vibrancy
when you feel
Crayola Gray.

I dare you
to wear bows in your hair
into your late thirties—
Timeless Taffeta.

I dare you to make
IQ haikus.
Be
test-score ridiculous.
Grade-A Grape.

I dare you
to be a syllable sage
color-outside-the-line meter.
Revolutionary Red.
I double dog dare you
To be
muddy-paw-print-on-the-floor rebellious.
Bulldog Brown.

Truth: It's ok
to be a remnant of water.
Something clear,
a tear, even.
Melancholy Stream.

But, I dare you to be
metabolic,
refusing to lineate,
daring to curl.
Twisted Tangerine.

I dare you to be
lightning-rod insane.
Thunderstrike Tempest.

I dare you to be
Dead-Leaf Crimson.
Monarch Orange.
Solar Pasture.

I dare
you to hold
hope like it's the last
hue. Final Shade.

insomnia

rebuff the purple skies and its indications to sleep.
sheep incantations grant me blanket amnesty.

Rosy-Cheeked

hydroplane through spring

uncouth and demoralized

                       as I hydroplane through spring.

     ersatz overalls

            waiting for june

   (and balmy skin).

sometimes
I guess

        I can be particularly

                         evasive

    line-swerving.

someone

               beyond

                     retrieval

    like a cannonball summer.

trucker-hat season is late to hit the highway.

                     Tant pis!

Lancee Whetman

how does one sow a miracle?

Finding satisfaction in landscapes should

    do the trick.

Short the fuse we call lightning—
it's

    a cactus lament.

The harshness
of an unplanned joke

    is ill-advised weather.

Neutrality is staying home.

    Toast
    with the lumberjack

who riles up

    your embers.

Pine after

    him
    and

smoldering hope.
Try not to undermine

    the Earth,

each other.
But I do them so **much harm**

    like I do unto myself.

I have to keep asking:
What are the odds that
tomorrow will come?
Infinite.

Flora

Rose. Honeysuckle. Birth plants of June. Symbols of beauty, love, honor, and devotion. Traits of which I do not have nor am willing to acquire. I am sidewalk-crack stem. Seedy. A weedy woman. Pithy. Blossom punch. In this invasive life, photosynthesis is a sin. I am shallow root. Wallflower shy. Dehydrated soul. Yellowing family frond. Surviving where you refuse to look. I am soiled expectation. I am Cyclamen. Resignation. Goodbye. I am Rue. Disdain. Regret. Possibly even ruin.

fiddlehead

xeriscape tears,
simple sadness
irrigating my cheeks.

this morning,
I find fiddleheads,
peeping up in clusters.
I say *thank you*, wondering
what I have to offer up
but an unfurling of fists.

rainy day runaway, droplets
apologizing for the weight
of gravity—I can barely
be upright.

stomaching too many
shadows, nauseating ink
that I write with.

*I want something
good, please.*
I welcome
a miracle.

April

It's mayhem, marching
into a month of aggregating

rain–the allure of spring.
The sunflowers keep

secrets, the rumor of seeds.
What rant to plant

this time? My soiled shoes
dilly dally delinquently.

It's the daytime
do's: shoot up saffron

root down in rutabaga.
We may or may not

be ready for June.
Hit jumpstart on summer.

Skip the good part—
the blooming—because

we don't know
if we deserve it.

roots

I fuss over fallen
trees,
the revelation of roots.
Imagine tension,
the tolerance of Earth.

Undermine attachments
to soil,
faulting no elemental force,
freeing the grip
of cross-hatching,
withdrawing from vertical,
abandoning nutrition.

Imagine standing
for centuries and being ok
with unstable gradient.
Wind—always taking
it out of you.

When it's time
to collapse,
it doesn't have to be
silent.

Rosy-Cheeked

spiders fly on Earth's electric-field currents

in search of an ionosphere vacation.
Me? I vacillate like some wind-current wayfarer.

This silk-propellant skin understands
the nature of ballooning

biology. Electrostatic brunette strands
bellow simple departures.

Like a flight-simulator spider,
I flit six-legged *sayonaras*.

There is a sense
I am just another creature

who wants
to leave.

all I hear are crickets

Entomology. Makes me a bit squeamish thinking about hexapoda. Six-legged fears of the

Animalia kingdom
Arthropoda phylum
Insecta class.

Nuptial gifts, like salivary foods, to copulate with pheromones.
Sex: males. They are soil suitors—larvae to lovers. Thorax sprung-wings. Nerve impulses, locomotion flapping, skyward stalwart.

Multigenerational migrations of locust plagues—a biblical reality: *They can travel up to 90 miles a day in swarms of 80 million,* the internet reports (and so does Exodus, as I proceed to exit Egypt). Aphid Armageddon.

The annual vulnerabilities of food-chain fungivores and herbaceous hosts. Sap sucker, plant zapper—all leaves are made of unequal tissue. Perennial nitrogen. Biochemical defenses—cyanogenic reactions to foliage. Call it: Predator toxification.

Create a colony, create a climate—ever-changing like our ecological exoskeletons. Molting to adulthood. *Shed it, silkworm!*

Queen bee. Bee castes, bee social, bee brood. Bee scared, honey bee. Humans prefer pollution > pollen.

Rosy-Cheeked

Specialist strategies. Generalist gumption. Adaptation is a challenge when you're digging dirt for free.

Phenological phenomena: the interdependence of species. What's a synonym for survival? Please don't say *resilience*.

Stop stepping on sidewalk ants: a series of stop-gap measures.

Beat the beetles (Beatles) to bed. Four (4) carabid runners down Abbey Road. Under evolution's influence, Child of Nature plays on the record-player, but all I hear tonight are crickets.

conspiratorial being

What do you believe in?
The woke
sky?

Chemical trails
are cloud pasteurization.
Divine providence
is the latest
bomb cyclone.

Strubbly weather
slamming the atmosphere.
Give me 24 hours
to intensify.

Have people believe
that I exist

(maybe).

Rosy-Cheeked

atlas heart

That's what my mother told me about Utah sandstone:
You find it in every corner of the world.

The land of red rock and juniper—
a place without humidity

and not much in terms of water reserves.
First in time. First in right.

The Lesser Goldfinch chirped
its morning correspondence.

We sipped piping-hot chamomile
took our toast on terracotta.

Flight
I feel more and more these days.

Weaning off of the West
for some time.

Too scared to ponder,
to wander elsewhere. Leave.

What would such an adventure entail?
I did not know.

But when I finally did leave
my desert nesting grounds
mama bird, sang:

Lancee Whetman

Fly my spirited child.
Carry that adobe heart with care.
Life is the changing-of-the-leaves.
Don't let your song of sand be snared.

The winds will take you where they must
Remnants of home, hold tight.
An atlas heart, you have
Now go, find your wings.
Live with all your might.

Botany

alpha—me—
beta-analyzing
how to train Howdy.
she chases after a ptarmigan
like it's all fun
and games.

Cody cracks a cool beer
atop the mountain—
binocular views.

we poke around the woods.
identify local flora.
he says:
remembering the difference
between watermelon berry stalks
and water hemlock
could save your life.

Lancee Whetman

The crane

In May, the migratory birds return. A sandhill crane lay, shot down on the tundra where I walked each morning.

Bright red forehead bill, covered in blood.
Olfactory spring can be fowl (foul).

It had just rained on the corpse: Death was undelayed that day. Decay's onset.

The catalyst of the crane's change: fungi.
On-scene saprotrophs steadily processing.

I plucked feathered remnants, placed its plumage on the brim of my Stetson as I mucked around the decomposition site.

The passage of time transpired, and so too, the sweat of my brow.
That summer lent itself to a whetted fall.

Reverence for autumn and all her fallen
leaves. That crane became skeletally serene. Corpse pose—

I laid next to the hulled-out frame. Fluidless,
it's evaporated entrails, gone.

An architectural display of bone.
Perpetually grounded.

My soles continued to walk there, that route, each day throughout the winter.

Rosy-Cheeked

The next spring, the cranes came back with their bugle calls rattling. Skyward. My visored hand enveloping shade.

I, looking up, see a six-foot wingspan.
Sun, silhouetting.

Lead pierced sky in an all-too familiar cycle.
The crane: Marsh-fallen.

Returning, like me, again and again, to this place.
Rotting, reborn.

hard, ships

I find stillness each morning
on these muddy banks
of the Wood River
and meditate on,
not much,
but more than those
who never meditate.

How can I
do more
for myself
and the world?

I don't know:
weather?
to remain?
The purest form
of truth-telling.
The sky whets me.
Place-determining
during a rainstorm
is hail on Earth.

Howdy and horsetail
at my ankles
angling me forward
to say farewells.

Fishermen off to
sea. See? Soon

hindsight brings hard-
ships into the harbor.

Loon. Attic.
I make out its call
clear the space out
for a loud dream.

I hear the warblers
the golden-crowned sparrows.
They want more from me.
A whistle, perhaps?
So do I.
But I don't know how
to leave
in song
or in silence.

It's June.
The time
to fish for food
a job, a heart
a life I want
to live.

dream job

tell me about the dream...where I make
enough money. where bills unfold

by the hundreds like a thin strip
teasing out of my twenties.

where pennies are no longer
pinched by sofa cushions.

the dream where it rains green
wallets. plump with paper

savings. savings. savings.
I take the "dream"

job with more
digits on the pay

check my welfare
mattress accounting—

am I happy or just
richer?

tell me about the dream
(job)—*where?*

Rosy-Cheeked migration

The winds beckon
a reaction from me.

The wild geese—
the biggest news around here.

There's relevance in migration.
Tern of the century

or just my craning thirties?
I'm on the brink of motion, too.

Part of the clique of ceremonial departures.
My warbled voice, my ruby-crowned tongue—

they fear the fledge.
Have I lost my godly wit?

Put me on the next sailing swan.
The thrush of my blush—

the only thing
that outlasts spring.

Lancee Whetman

beating around the bush

what's my next move? how should I know?
I am beating around the bush, most things,

like staying in this Alaskan village that
has held my fishing-poled dreams,

snagging one last prodigal
summer. better make

the most of it. a rainy spring sure knows
how to demoralize. let these legs run

a few miles down the bike path to the boat
launch. second-guessing the guy.

a divergence of decisions, a **foray** of
the future, frustrates me, **this** life.

soon, you'll find me staggering at
the sight of the midnight

sun.

a mountain of lost hope
& some herring
in hand.

Rosy-Cheeked

two weeks' notice

Trade the Last Frontier for pura vida,
swap frostbite for salt air,
an inbox for a passport—
destination: somewhere I've never been.

Off the beaten path, I go,
before I become a 9-to-5 sociopath.
Enough micromanage,
more microgreens.
Maracuyá makes me passionate
about living again.

Fruit is fresh,
like my tendency to dream.
Tweak this. Teak that.
Was riptide. Was ruckus.
Now I'm gone with the flow,
with the current-ly.

Bullshit. Bullfrog. Bullion.
Worth every penny—every colón.
Hablo un poquito de español,
and a whole lot of
throwing-in-the-towel.

moving sale

Sell the barstools—
I don't need them.
Nor the boot dryer,
the yoga ball,
the bed sheets.

Take what you want.
Half-off.
Even the rest
of the half-and-half.
I can't carry it all
in this tote,
this bag.

The toaster still works.
So does the shotgun.
Just make sure you load
each with the right ammo—
one's for bread,
the other
for shells
for bears and birds.

Nick nacks go
for four cents.
Little treasures
from the last town.
Take what's left
of me.
This is the torture of moving:

Rosy-Cheeked

buying less,
saying *goodbye*
more.

The day after I quit

my job, I made minestrone soup and health-conscious bird bars that I tried to pass as "cookies" to my partner. He knew I was lying (and crumbling) like I was when I said I could stay in that job until March. A decision, a right one, feels like peace. And that's how it felt to wake up today. My pillows sang a well-rested chorus. There was satisfaction in not defining myself as failure. No ass-ridden state. Just steps, skips, sprints forward. No belittlement by a boss. No telephonic-ringing-off-the-hook insanity. No windowless office. No more holding on by a hinge. No compromising. No more. There was the penance of making phone calls to family I'd neglected. There was time. Time to bring lunch to my elderly neighbor and talk about wood stain, woodpeckers. Time to shoot hoops at the local gym. Time for vacuuming the apartment—all of it. There was time. Then, an arrival. An email about a carpentry-training application I sent months ago. There was an acceptance. There had been ice fog all week, which finally lifted. I thought, *I'd really like to build doors.*

Rosy-Cheeked

the interview | the in-between

Ask me all the questions.
I get peppered with:
What is the difference between a bribe
& a facilitation payment?
I see you have "psychic readings"
& brewing kombucha
in the hobbies section
of your resume…?

Coming off of three hours
of sleep after
Howdy's late-night
bear-confrontation
and barking soirée,
the interview is an hour-and-a-half
of me thinking, *damn,*
I can see myself working here,
which is the first time in months
I've felt committal to
a job
a place
an idea that wasn't all
imposter
& independence.

I decompress
my stress

& my morning
mattress back
with some downward
dog, as Howdy hits REM.
Joker-smile birthmark,
freebie pup,
village mutt,
byproduct of a non-spayed
dog population.
The Wild West has no vets.
We both don't want
kids (for now).
I leave room for the idea
that biology may kick in soon
but my mat & mind
say it's time for savasana.

I write a list of alternative ways
to describe a pothole:
avoidance swerve
irregular depression
tax-payer problem
tired rut
road bowl
street cavity
unexpected   ditch
gravel bunker
axel hell
dirt gouge
dirt gorge
maintained neglect
neglectfully maintained.

Call it "runjour."

Rosy-Cheeked

It's like skijour,
but now your pet pulls
you miles on concrete
(instead of snow).

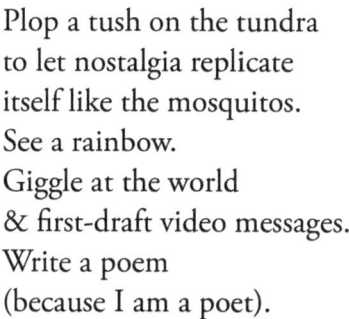

Plop a tush on the tundra
to let nostalgia replicate
itself like the mosquitos.
See a rainbow.
Giggle at the world
& first-draft video messages.
Write a poem
(because I am a poet).

Today, I quacked like
a Dillingham duck
because all I was guilty of
was breaking stained glass,
almost my own heart—
that slippery crimson.

tumbleweed

Stop the electrical power
to the apartment.
Refill the fuel tank.
Turn in the P.O. box key.
Leave a forwarding address
(if there is one).

It won't be the last time I do this:
wind-shifting, flight-taking,
chasing the promise of a new adventure.

I am all tumbleweed—
taking the path of least resistance
(even when it resists me first).

Call it maturity,
this Alaskan departure.
I let go of roots,
carried by a spring breeze
from soil that held me
for four exact, undefined years.

I won't try to make it final.
I won't try to call it
a conclusion.
Instead, I scatter seeds—
pieces of me—
this poem, for instance.

I loved Appalachia,

then adobe and desert even more
until I met the northern lights
the spawning salmon,
the silence of a western sky.
The place that I played
with the idea of staying
for a while
(maybe forever).

But I am tired.
Road-worn.
Dusty.
Half-empty,
full-hearted,
a starting-anew woman.

I am the phenomenon
of detaching,
and rolling—
on,
and on,
and on.

hi Anchorage

It's been a minute since I clutched
too tightly—
to a few bags,
to a new beginning.
Sweaty in an airport,
it must be that three-year cycle of mine—
weaning off from the wandering
wounds.

Last time, I left you
to digress from downtowns,
to find some sweet survival
in the bush.
Here, I'm a pedestrian.
There, I felt
a definition of place.
I know comparisons
between here and there
are unkind,
how I attribute worth
differently depending
on geography.
My assumptions can be so naive,
but a novelty, too.

Today, my stomach flipped
in turbulence.
Metaphors always
make me sick at 10,000 feet.
The sky has that

sobering effect.

Anchorage,
Pinch me like March did.
Pucker your lips
like spring rain.
Let me wane—
wishing I made
no mistake.

But what I mean to say,
Anchorage,
is maybe in time,
you could feel like there, too?
A soft place
to land.
Soon (if possible).

howdy, partner

I'm just a provision
from some flickering

old western. Still haunted
by the last Alaskan cowboy

standoff. Revolvers
stay holstered.

It took just one shot—
unorthodox,

but defining. To be flawed—
like me—follows

distinct trajectories. I've mastered
the art of misdirected meanings, dictionary

crimes with no correction. Peeling off
another age layer. Falsify

the sunset's softest pastels. Make
palpable again, the nights

 alone. Correspond
with the alcohol. Ask

my backbone where the hell
it has been lately. Try,

Rosy-Cheeked

just try, to tend to the simple.
Resuscitate the soil from last year's

garden. Provoke the sunflowers
to finally ascend.

rattlesnake

The incongruence of a coil—
a continuous prediction of mishaps.
Mastication and the spread of camouflage—
everything hidden, everything chewed.

I'm strapped by the breeze
and its reverse architecture.
Broken investments—
nightmare venom, slow-release.

Look at me through my glasses.
To suffer is to see you
in sharp relief—
magnified,
blurred.

The past is a patient patient.
I miss Miss Desert—
all her rattles and charm,
her sinister rhythm,
her warning signs.

What does it feel like to have scale?
To carry fang derangement?
To slither with ambition?

If only I had such conviction—
to bite back
before becoming.

Rosy-Cheeked

prayers to Hemingway

I guess I'm foolish enough
to eclipse. The sky must be marvelous

conjecture as I look up into oblivion.
Reciting the constellations, by name

as if I committed them to memory
of the multiverse's ever-multiplying

effect. Well, hell
can be quite persuasive

when staring into heaven.
It's a Catch-22—trading halos

for ball caps, capsizing
my childhood time capsule.

Forgotten, twenty years
too late—remnants of a sunny

afternoon. I'll keep
spinning in orbit—

the gravity of an acorn scorns
my noggin'—not again!
Rounded too many suns:
cosmic dizzy spells

from dust, particulate

responsibilities, vertigo trauma.

Lost in a diabolical desert
hoping the sands of time disband

my grainy sin. we are
savants of climate

chaos. Gurus of a generation
bound by a blighted sea,

rigging metaphors to the sails:
long-winded hope. I guess

I am trying to nix my nihilism—
a never-ending dismantling

of my mantle, volcano lust.
Come bust (combust) to the end

together. I guess
by writing these place-based poems

I still pray to Hemmingway
that the demands of this age

don't get the best
of me.

Rosy-Cheeked

ice cream & sunscreen

Drip-dry summer. Bad Bunny intoxication.
Pop-punk popsicles on our tongues full of UV rays.

Tanned-skin goals.
Park-loop innocence.

Wanton & willing for midnight
and its stardom simplicity.

Grass in our jeans,
jokes, too.

That season of sheer jubilance
was purely ours.

deep gratitude

Snow wagon of the sky.
Our village's bush pilot drops us
at Lake Beverley—
an unoccupied valley,
save for wolverine tracks
and rabbit prints,
awaiting our adrenaline-fueled arrival.

Our planks transition—
back-and-forthing
between friction's ascent
and glide's steady plunge.

A hard-packed pit,
good practice.
Shovel-dug ice bricks
ease avalanche concerns
in a place where triggers lurk—
but we've got an aptitude
(and altitude)
for safe expeditions.

Surface floating,
zooming across frozen water dust,
the landscape amphitheater sings
a song of silence—
our favorite soundtrack.

Paint-brush-stroked turns,
a few splattered imprints

Rosy-Cheeked

from my snow-angel Gore-Tex gear—
call it contemporary mountain art.

And at the end,
to honor what it truly means
to get "out there,"
slugs of off-brand Fireball
glissade down our throats—
merriment and merry-weather libations.

These ski lines,
untraced by humans (to my knowledge),
deserve an honorary title.

I call the route:
Deep Gratitude.

I share the trail

because the path
was never meant
for me alone.

I share the trail
with porcupine, barbing its quills,
with moose, pressing hooves into earth,
with bald eagle, just fledging its nest.

I share the trail
with Howdy, curious
at all the above—
all the wild,
restless motion.

I share the trail
with season,
with sunrise,
with surprise encounter.

I share the trail
with heart, steadying its pace.
With ancestors,
with songbird,
with rainy day,
with mud.
At sea level,
at 14,000 feet (and rising),
I share the trail
with unknown feats

Rosy-Cheeked

and fears still waiting
to be reckoned with.

I share the trail
with avalanche,
with blizzard,
with boughing branch
and huckleberry bush.

I share a lichen-ing laugh,
lend an earlobe to chickadee,
singing:
You're going the right way.

March, make me

raise my hackles at the hurt.
Howl at the happenings
he did after dark.
March, make me rattle
on. Froth at the mouth
for the truth. Shatter a lung
while unearthing it.

March, make me yearn—
for the bloom, for the best years ahead.
Make my rage dissipate into flowers.
My bouquet hands haven't held trust
for a while. Why did he feel
like thistle
instead of tulip
when touched?
Always distraught by Narcissus—
that damned daffodil.

March, make me want—
both love and lavender.
Make me stir without alarm,
make me lighten, please.
Make me lurch
forward into a good deed,
a good book,
a good cry.
Let me lounge, look up,
find the astronomical—
the Blood Moon will suffice.

Rosy-Cheeked

March, make me into something
less fleeting:
less tide,
less idle.
Embolden me—
to ask a stranger out,
to disregard the consequences
of caring too much,
to send novels of texts,
untimid, all-too-timely,
ten seconds after receipt.
To put on a bathing suit,
plunge (at least partly)
into an ice-cold lake.
To play *You Make Me Feel Like Dancing*
by Leo Sayer at the day's sunny onset.

March, oh my dearest March,
make me, me again—
two left feet
and all.

Lancee Whetman

the river

Predestiny is

        a shore,

            a sanctuary.

The sand tells the time

of passing grains.

            The big-to-small theory—

                stones skip on tension.

        Do we, too?

Tip-toe rush.

        Tranquility is submerged.

              Do we dare follow

        bathing

        suit?

ode to the little things

Here's to reviving minor pleasures—
a slow sidewalk strut,
reading smut,
saying *I'm from SL,UT*
(Salt Lake City, Utah)
with a wink.

Picking up rubbish.
Migrating to the mountains
(more or less).

Here's to jest as the best coping mechanism,
hips slanted just right to show sass.
Here's to being a double-dip mastermind,
dunking Oreos…twice,
milk mustaches
straight out of the commercials.

Here's to planting understanding
in this year's garden,
auctioning off level-headedness
for a single day of recklessness,
wrestling my lips with someone loving,
and catching the flash
of gray beluga backs in the bay—
just when I least expected it.

to be happy

My, oh my,

    have you seen

        the moonlight
recently?

Have you smelled all of

        the roadside daisies that you could?
            Let your

laughter lift up

    to the heavens;

        tell the angels that you

had the best

    goddamn day

        down here on Earth.

    Get lost

in the best novel,

        a lollipop,

a Pablo Picasso painting.

        Put your hand
    over your heart

and swear that this feeling
    will

        last.

Rosy-Cheeked nomad

I'm all slipped
middle finger,
flipped adverb,
all *uck fumble.

I'm unfinished business,
a casualty
of flimsy conscience,
una ola pequeña
learning the science
of walking on water.

Religiously spiritual
about a good view
and uneven concrete.
Atlas ballerina.
Backroads biathlete.

I am all mediocrity—
minor tweak,
major twang,
a trellis of geography.

Small-town ambiance,
big-city mess.
I'm all birch,
bark,
bitch.
Red-lipstick sane,
blaming myself for potholes.

I am tugboat,
flightless-bird cliché,
twiddling thumbs,
hitchhiker lost,
daring myself to stand
in unfamiliar territory.

the wanting of being

I don't want my smile
to be a mere formality.
I don't want a personality
without pretense.

It is a privilege to write,
to hold in my hands
what I become.

I want to slacken
my pace
a bit.
Walk with time
(and then some).

I don't want to trip
over my own backbone.
I want my only dream
to be existing
in the universe.

loop

To go around in circles
can be insanity—
or infinity.
We keep on,
loop de loop,
hula-hooping,
wheel-turning.

Can you bare your soul?
Lend a quarter of your mind?
Clockwork, we arrive
on time—
(even when we're late).

The brown dirt
is only as lonesome
as the last drifter
who walked it—
flipped thumb,
tipped hat,
bitten nail,
pulse-thump.

Poems have only one "o,"
just like "world."
Blue-marble Earth,
a beautiful beaded beatitude.
Both tremble.
Earthquake words.
Relax, little rambler.

Rosy-Cheeked

Give 'em a sunbow,
a namaste,
a never again.

By all measure,
accept your roundness,
the heavy pack,
the missed train
for all that it is—
and all that it isn't.

Lancee Whetman

my advice?

Order the special of the day.
Howl at the moon.
Run until you feel your pulse—
your heart,
your aliveness.
Become electricity.
Something bright—
like the moon,
like the sun,
like dandelions scattering into the wind.
Cross the lover's threshold
be poised, be psychedelic,
bemuse others
bewilder yourself.
Catch 5 a.m. by the tail.
Tell it *good morning*.
Translate your grogginess
into the language of coffee.
Salivate over a sunrise.
Careen where the wind
takes you. Shake the moment's
hand like it's the deal
of the century.

Rosy-Cheeked

the beauty of sticking around

For the buzz of morning dew. The sacrament that is sunrise. For the symphony of your own laugh ricochetting off of a canyon. The warmth of your pulse. It is a feat to feel the breeze bellow: *Stay*. It swirls around you.

fox, robin, mosquito

The fabulous trio
I meet on my morning walk.
They chatter, scamper, buzz,
through today's lush hush.

It's real—
this sun—
I lather sunscreen on my bum.
Chirp, chirp—
purge a soda-pop burp.

Spring sings—
can you hear its golden ring?
I can't stop this hop,
this wild body bop.
I'm on the astral plane,
Plain Jane, delightfully insane.

The stars are all lookalikes.
There goes the air from the tire on my bike!
Oh well—
it's still swell—
the way the girthy soil smells.

It's a worm,
as I learn
To wriggle, to writhe,
To live before these days slip by.

It's nature—ain't it neat?

Rosy-Cheeked

Look! A bee on my skirt pleat.
I snap my fingers,
hope this joy just lingers
a little while longer…
before the sun folds into slumber—
like us,
and our beautiful, cosmic,
human dust.

adventure

Don't call the sun a shame.
Tidy up

                                          the picnic blanket.
                                                  Reject

routine.
Go ascend
like athlete.

                                                  Release

sweat.
Call upon the moon.
It is a relief
to be spellbound.
Unsure of

                                                  direction.

Your path is

                                             not fiction—
                                                    it is
                                                      fire,

fuel,

                                           grass-stained.

Tally ho!

                                          The send off

is the hardest part.

Rosy-Cheeked

green lake

You remember the avalanche lily?
The stop-and-smell-the-roses attitude
we had that summer?
Milk thistle
and milk shakes?

We appreciated the shade most
when the sun gave us too much light
than we knew what to do with.

All we wanted were roses,
to recite the poems we knew best,
baseball-mitt success,
the making of heart-shaped

a
    n
        y
           t
               h
                  i
                     n
                        g
                           s
                            .

era

There's an itch at 29—waiting for 30. For a refreshing
ten years after disappointments. The twenties can pucker

our faces from such sour-packed lessons. We can't say
we didn't put up a fight (even though we should have

held our tongues). New beginnings, perhaps a change
in age, are like snail mail. Takes time,

but is so meaningful when it arrives at the door.
It's almost as if you're watching the dawn tip

toe into a rosy dress, blush, then say,
it's going to be a good ~~day~~ decade.

Rosy-Cheeked

dear human

Tear the curtains from the wall
for summer is yawning

at you. Dear human,
I have much to say

earthen as I am.
This morning is break

-ing
better than you

have ever seen
before.

A promise
little darling

dew awaits you.
Camouflage yourself

in chamomile
(if necessary).

Daylight is
girthy.

The grass is
tickled

pink. Roses, drop
thorns

to bouquet
your hand.

You are
seed. Deep

soil.
Bright wings.

All things
great.

Grandeur.

acknowledgements

No rose blooms in isolation—its growth is shaped by the hands that tend to it. *Rosy-Cheeked* would not have become what it is without the care, insight, and patience of those who helped nurture it along the way. To my editors, Zachary Olson and Lucas Street—thank you for pruning where needed, for watering the words that mattered. To my formatter, Kristina Konstantinova, and my cover artist, Grace Su, for ensuring this collection grew into its fullest form. And to my beta readers—Kristina Percy and Caroline Smith—thank you for being the first to wander through this garden of poetry, for your thoughtful feedback, and for reminding me that even the thorniest lines have their place. Your encouragement has been a sunlight all its own. This book, like any wild and wonderful thing, is better because of you all.

Lancee Whetman

about the author

Lancee Whetman is a poet, storyteller, and forever-curious human. When she isn't observing the world through rose-colored glasses and writing about it, Lancee can be found doing yoga, spending time with her dog, Howdy, and taking gentle walks amongst prickly pear cacti. She is the author of *Blinded by Feeling* (2023), *Further West & Fireweed* (2024), and *Chapped Lips* (2025).